BALANCE SUMMARY

Month	Yr	Total Income (Box B)	Total Out-goings (Box D)	Balance Column E (B minus D)	Mon...			...E ...D)
Annual Total					Annual Total			

How to use this Book

» Step 1. Begin each month with the EXPENDITURE Table

i.   Use the spare columns to add any extra categories.

ii. If you would like to enter budgets for each category, enter these in the top row of the table.

iii. Throughout the month, log each expenditure in a new row. Enter amounts directly into the category columns. Use the calendar for reminders such as bills.

iv. At the end of the month, total each category's expenditure in the second row of the table (directly beneath any budgets for easy comparison). Sum all the individual category totals to find your Total Expenditure for the month and enter it in Box A.

» Step 2. Fill in the INCOME Table

For all months except the first, the Balance Brought Forward entry refers to the Balance from the previous month, which can be found in column E (above). Bear in mind that it may be negative. For the first month you may wish to enter the sum of any household petty-cash and any unallocated monies in current / checking accounts.

The Others category may include, for example, pension income, bonuses, gifts, inheritances, capital gains or state support.

» Step 3. Fill in the OUTGOINGS Table

Transfer the Total Expenditure (calculated in Step 1) from Box A into the first box.

The Other category may include, for example, pension contributions and personal taxes.

Subtotalling the first four categories will give you your 'committed' outgoings in Box C. You can now compare this figure to your Total Income (Box B) and make any allocations to the Savings Logs at the back of the book before computing your Total Outgoings in Box D.

» Step 4. Find your Net Balance for the month

Transfer your Total Income (Box B) and your Total Outgoings (Box D) to the Balance Summary above and enter the difference in Column E.

MONTH	YEAR

- ○ ....
- ○ ....
- ○ ....
- ○ ....
- ○ ....
- ○ ....

INCOME

Balance brought forward (From front page)	
Pay 1	
Pay 2	
Interest from Investments/Savings	
Others	
Total	Box B

OUTGOINGS

Expenditure (From Box A below)	
Mortgage or Rent	
Loan / Credit Card Payments	
Other	
Subtotal	Box C
To Savings 1	
To Savings 2	
Total	Box D

EXPENDITURE

Budgets →

Totals | Box A

Item	Date	Receipt?	Cleared	Household								Health				
				(1) Insurance	(2) Maintenance	(3) Utilities	(4) Cable/TV Internet/Phone	(5) Furnishings	(6) Property Tax	(7) Groceries	(8) Laundry & Cleaning	(9) Life & Health Insurance	(10) Medical, Dental & Eye Care	(11) Exercise	(12) Medicines	(13) Vacations

CALENDAR

MON	TUE	WED	THU	FRI	SAT	SUN

Transport				Dependents				Personal					Giving					
(14)	(15)	(16)	(17)	(18)	(19)	(20)	(21)	(22)	(23)	(24)	(25)	(26)	(27)	(28)	(29)	(30)	(31)	(32)
Tickets & Passes	Vehicle tax & maintenance	Fuel	Vehicle Insurance	Care Fees	Day-to-Day Needs	Allowance	Activities	Technology	Clothing	Pastimes	Toiletries & Bodycare	Leisure	Gifts	Charity				

EXPENDITURE				Household								Health				
				(1)	(2)	(3)	(4)	(5)	(6)	(7)	(8)	(9)	(10)	(11)	(12)	(13)
Item	Date	Receipt?	Cleared	Insurance	Maintenance	Utilities	Cable/TV Internet/Phone	Furnishings	Property Tax	Groceries	Laundry & Cleaning	Life & Health Insurance	Medical, Dental & Eye Care	Exercise	Medicines	Vacations

(14)	(15)	(16)	(17)	(18)	(19)	(20)	(21)	(22)	(23)	(24)	(25)	(26)	(27)	(28)	(29)	(30)	(31)	(32)
Transport				**Dependents**				**Personal**					**Giving**					
Tickets & Passes	Vehicle tax & maintenance	Fuel	Vehicle Insurance	Care Fees	Day-to-Day Needs	Allowance	Activities	Technology	Clothing	Pastimes	Toiletries & Bodycare	Leisure	Gifts	Charity				

MONTH	YEAR

INCOME		OUTGOINGS	
Balance brought forward (From front page)		Expenditure (From Box A below)	
Pay 1		Mortgage or Rent	
Pay 2		Loan / Credit Card Payments	
Interest from Investments/Savings		Other	
Others		Subtotal	Box C
		To Savings 1	
		To Savings 2	
Total	Box B	Total	Box D

○ ....
○ ....
○ ....
○ ....
○ ....
○ ....

EXPENDITURE

Budgets →

Totals | Box A

Household

Health

Item	Date	Receipt?	Cleared	(1) Insurance	(2) Maintenance	(3) Utilities	(4) Cable/TV Internet/Phone	(5) Furnishings	(6) Property Tax	(7) Groceries	(8) Laundry & Cleaning	(9) Life & Health Insurance	(10) Medical, Dental & Eye Care	(11) Exercise	(12) Medicines	(13) Vacations

CALENDAR

MON	TUE	WED	THU	FRI	SAT	SUN

Transport				Dependents				Personal					Giving					
(14)	(15)	(16)	(17)	(18)	(19)	(20)	(21)	(22)	(23)	(24)	(25)	(26)	(27)	(28)	(29)	(30)	(31)	(32)
Tickets & Passes	Vehicle tax & maintenance	Fuel	Vehicle Insurance	Care Fees	Day-to-Day Needs	Allowance	Activities	Technology	Clothing	Pastimes	Toiletries & Bodycare	Leisure	Gifts	Charity				

EXPENDITURE				Household								Health				
				(1)	(2)	(3)	(4)	(5)	(6)	(7)	(8)	(9)	(10)	(11)	(12)	(13)
Item	Date	Receipt?	Cleared	Insurance	Maintenance	Utilities	Cable/TV Internet/Phone	Furnishings	Property Tax	Groceries	Laundry & Cleaning	Life & Health Insurance	Medical, Dental & Eye Care	Exercise	Medicines	Vacations

(14)	(15)	(16)	(17)	(18)	(19)	(20)	(21)	(22)	(23)	(24)	(25)	(26)	(27)	(28)	(29)	(30)	(31)	(32)
Transport				Dependents				Personal					Giving					
Tickets & Passes	Vehicle tax & maintenance	Fuel	Vehicle Insurance	Care Fees	Day-to-Day Needs	Allowance	Activities	Technology	Clothing	Pastimes	Toiletries & Bodycare	Leisure	Gifts	Charity				
(14)	(15)	(16)	(17)	(18)	(19)	(20)	(21)	(22)	(23)	(24)	(25)	(26)	(27)	(28)	(29)	(30)	(31)	(32)

MONTH	YEAR

INCOME		OUTGOINGS	
Balance brought forward (From front page)		Expenditure (From Box A below)	
Pay 1		Mortgage or Rent	
Pay 2		Loan / Credit Card Payments	
Interest from Investments/Savings		Other	
Others		Subtotal	Box C
		To Savings 1	
		To Savings 2	
	Total	Box B	Total	Box D

EXPENDITURE

Budgets →

Totals | Box A

Item	Date	Receipt?	Cleared	Household								Health				
				(1) Insurance	(2) Maintenance	(3) Utilities	(4) Cable/TV Internet/Phone	(5) Furnishings	(6) Property Tax	(7) Groceries	(8) Laundry & Cleaning	(9) Life & Health Insurance	(10) Medical, Dental & Eye Care	(11) Exercise	(12) Medicines	(13) Vacations

CALENDAR

MON	TUE	WED	THU	FRI	SAT	SUN

Transport				Dependents				Personal					Giving					
(14)	(15)	(16)	(17)	(18)	(19)	(20)	(21)	(22)	(23)	(24)	(25)	(26)	(27)	(28)	(29)	(30)	(31)	(32)
Tickets & Passes	Vehicle tax & maintenance	Fuel	Vehicle Insurance	Care Fees	Day-to-Day Needs	Allowance	Activities	Technology	Clothing	Pastimes	Toiletries & Bodycare	Leisure	Gifts	Charity				

EXPENDITURE				Household								Health				
Item	Date	Receipt?	Cleared	(1) Insurance	(2) Maintenance	(3) Utilities	(4) Cable/TV Internet/Phone	(5) Furnishings	(6) Property Tax	(7) Groceries	(8) Laundry & Cleaning	(9) Life & Health Insurance	(10) Medical, Dental & Eye Care	(11) Exercise	(12) Medicines	(13) Vacations

Transport				Dependents				Personal					Giving					
(14)	(15)	(16)	(17)	(18)	(19)	(20)	(21)	(22)	(23)	(24)	(25)	(26)	(27)	(28)	(29)	(30)	(31)	(32)
Tickets & Passes	Vehicle tax & maintenance	Fuel	Vehicle Insurance	Care Fees	Day-to-Day Needs	Allowance	Activities	Technology	Clothing	Pastimes	Toiletries & Bodycare	Leisure	Gifts	Charity				
(14)	(15)	(16)	(17)	(18)	(19)	(20)	(21)	(22)	(23)	(24)	(25)	(26)	(27)	(28)	(29)	(30)	(31)	(32)

MONTH	YEAR

○ _____

○ _____

○ _____

○ _____

○ _____

○ _____

INCOME		OUTGOINGS	
Balance brought forward (From front page)		Expenditure (From Box A below)	
Pay 1		Mortgage or Rent	
Pay 2		Loan / Credit Card Payments	
Interest from Investments/Savings		Other	
Others		Subtotal	Box C
		To Savings 1	
		To Savings 2	
Total	Box B	Total	Box D

EXPENDITURE

Budgets →

Totals | Box A

Item	Date	Receipt?	Cleared	Household								Health				
				(1) Insurance	(2) Maintenance	(3) Utilities	(4) Cable/TV Internet/Phone	(5) Furnishings	(6) Property Tax	(7) Groceries	(8) Laundry & Cleaning	(9) Life & Health Insurance	(10) Medical, Dental & Eye Care	(11) Exercise	(12) Medicines	(13) Vacations

CALENDAR

MON	TUE	WED	THU	FRI	SAT	SUN

Transport				Dependents				Personal					Giving					
(14)	(15)	(16)	(17)	(18)	(19)	(20)	(21)	(22)	(23)	(24)	(25)	(26)	(27)	(28)	(29)	(30)	(31)	(32)
Tickets & Passes	Vehicle tax & maintenance	Fuel	Vehicle Insurance	Care Fees	Day-to-Day Needs	Allowance	Activities	Technology	Clothing	Pastimes	Toiletries & Bodycare	Leisure	Gifts	Charity				

EXPENDITURE				Household								Health				
Item	Date	Receipt?	Cleared	(1) Insurance	(2) Maintenance	(3) Utilities	(4) Cable/TV Internet/Phone	(5) Furnishings	(6) Property Tax	(7) Groceries	(8) Laundry & Cleaning	(9) Life & Health Insurance	(10) Medical, Dental & Eye Care	(11) Exercise	(12) Medicines	(13) Vacations

(14)	(15)	(16)	(17)	(18)	(19)	(20)	(21)	(22)	(23)	(24)	(25)	(26)	(27)	(28)	(29)	(30)	(31)	(32)
Transport				Dependents				Personal					Giving					
Tickets & Passes	Vehicle tax & maintenance	Fuel	Vehicle Insurance	Care Fees	Day-to-Day Needs	Allowance	Activities	Technology	Clothing	Pastimes	Toiletries & Bodycare	Leisure	Gifts	Charity				

MONTH	YEAR

○ _____
○ _____
○ _____
○ _____
○ _____

INCOME		OUTGOINGS	
Balance brought forward (From front page)		Expenditure (From Box A below)	
Pay 1		Mortgage or Rent	
Pay 2		Loan / Credit Card Payments	
Interest from Investments/Savings		Other	
Others		Subtotal	Box C
		To Savings 1	
		To Savings 2	
Total	Box B	Total	Box D

EXPENDITURE

Budgets →

Totals | Box A |

	Household								Health				
	(1)	(2)	(3)	(4)	(5)	(6)	(7)	(8)	(9)	(10)	(11)	(12)	(13)
Item / Date / Receipt? / Cleared	Insurance	Maintenance	Utilities	Cable/TV Internet/Phone	Furnishings	Property Tax	Groceries	Laundry & Cleaning	Life & Health Insurance	Medical, Dental & Eye Care	Exercise	Medicines	Vacations

CALENDAR

MON	TUE	WED	THU	FRI	SAT	SUN

Transport				Dependents				Personal					Giving					
(14)	(15)	(16)	(17)	(18)	(19)	(20)	(21)	(22)	(23)	(24)	(25)	(26)	(27)	(28)	(29)	(30)	(31)	(32)
Tickets & Passes	Vehicle tax & maintenance	Fuel	Vehicle Insurance	Care Fees	Day-to-Day Needs	Allowance	Activities	Technology	Clothing	Pastimes	Toiletries & Bodycare	Leisure	Gifts	Charity				

EXPENDITURE				Household								Health				
Item	Date	Receipt?	Cleared	(1) Insurance	(2) Maintenance	(3) Utilities	(4) Cable/TV Internet/Phone	(5) Furnishings	(6) Property Tax	(7) Groceries	(8) Laundry & Cleaning	(9) Life & Health Insurance	(10) Medical, Dental & Eye Care	(11) Exercise	(12) Medicines	(13) Vacations

Transport				Dependents				Personal					Giving					
(14)	(15)	(16)	(17)	(18)	(19)	(20)	(21)	(22)	(23)	(24)	(25)	(26)	(27)	(28)	(29)	(30)	(31)	(32)
Tickets & Passes	Vehicle tax & maintenance	Fuel	Vehicle Insurance	Care Fees	Day-to-Day Needs	Allowance	Activities	Technology	Clothing	Pastimes	Toiletries & Bodycare	Leisure	Gifts	Charity				

MONTH	YEAR

○ ....

○ ....

○ ....

○ ....

○ ....

○ ....

INCOME		OUTGOINGS	
Balance brought forward (From front page)		Expenditure (From Box A below)	
Pay 1		Mortgage or Rent	
Pay 2		Loan / Credit Card Payments	
Interest from Investments/Savings		Other	
Others		Subtotal	Box C
		To Savings 1	
		To Savings 2	
Total	Box B	Total	Box D

EXPENDITURE

Budgets →

Totals | Box A

Item	Date	Receipt?	Cleared	Household								Health				
				(1) Insurance	(2) Maintenance	(3) Utilities	(4) Cable/TV Internet/Phone	(5) Furnishings	(6) Property Tax	(7) Groceries	(8) Laundry & Cleaning	(9) Life & Health Insurance	(10) Medical, Dental & Eye Care	(11) Exercise	(12) Medicines	(13) Vacations

CALENDAR

MON	TUE	WED	THU	FRI	SAT	SUN

Transport				Dependents				Personal					Giving					
(14)	(15)	(16)	(17)	(18)	(19)	(20)	(21)	(22)	(23)	(24)	(25)	(26)	(27)	(28)	(29)	(30)	(31)	(32)
Tickets & Passes	Vehicle tax & maintenance	Fuel	Vehicle Insurance	Care Fees	Day-to-Day Needs	Allowance	Activities	Technology	Clothing	Pastimes	Toiletries & Bodycare	Leisure	Gifts	Charity				

EXPENDITURE				Household								Health				
Item	Date	Receipt?	Cleared	(1) Insurance	(2) Maintenance	(3) Utilities	(4) Cable/TV Internet/Phone	(5) Furnishings	(6) Property Tax	(7) Groceries	(8) Laundry & Cleaning	(9) Life & Health Insurance	(10) Medical, Dental & Eye Care	(11) Exercise	(12) Medicines	(13) Vacations

Transport				Dependents				Personal					Giving					
(14)	(15)	(16)	(17)	(18)	(19)	(20)	(21)	(22)	(23)	(24)	(25)	(26)	(27)	(28)	(29)	(30)	(31)	(32)
Tickets & Passes	Vehicle tax & maintenance	Fuel	Vehicle Insurance	Care Fees	Day-to-Day Needs	Allowance	Activities	Technology	Clothing	Pastimes	Toiletries & Bodycare	Leisure	Gifts	Charity				
(14)	(15)	(16)	(17)	(18)	(19)	(20)	(21)	(22)	(23)	(24)	(25)	(26)	(27)	(28)	(29)	(30)	(31)	(32)

MONTH	YEAR

INCOME		OUTGOINGS	
Balance brought forward (From front page)		Expenditure (From Box A below)	
Pay 1		Mortgage or Rent	
Pay 2		Loan / Credit Card Payments	
Interest from Investments/Savings		Other	
Others		Subtotal	Box C
		To Savings 1	
		To Savings 2	
Total	Box B	Total	Box D

EXPENDITURE		Household								Health				
Budgets →														
Totals	Box A													
Item	Date	Receipt?	Cleared	(1) Insurance	(2) Maintenance	(3) Utilities	(4) Cable/TV Internet/Phone	(5) Furnishings	(6) Property Tax	(7) Groceries	(8) Laundry & Cleaning	(9) Life & Health Insurance	(10) Medical, Dental & Eye Care	(11) Exercise	(12) Medicines	(13) Vacations

CALENDAR

MON	TUE	WED	THU	FRI	SAT	SUN

Transport				Dependents				Personal					Giving					
(14)	(15)	(16)	(17)	(18)	(19)	(20)	(21)	(22)	(23)	(24)	(25)	(26)	(27)	(28)	(29)	(30)	(31)	(32)
Tickets & Passes	Vehicle tax & maintenance	Fuel	Vehicle Insurance	Care Fees	Day-to-Day Needs	Allowance	Activities	Technology	Clothing	Pastimes	Toiletries & Bodycare	Leisure	Gifts	Charity				

EXPENDITURE				Household								Health				
Item	Date	Receipt?	Cleared	(1) Insurance	(2) Maintenance	(3) Utilities	(4) Cable/TV Internet/Phone	(5) Furnishings	(6) Property Tax	(7) Groceries	(8) Laundry & Cleaning	(9) Life & Health Insurance	(10) Medical, Dental & Eye Care	(11) Exercise	(12) Medicines	(13) Vacations

(14)	(15)	(16)	(17)	(18)	(19)	(20)	(21)	(22)	(23)	(24)	(25)	(26)	(27)	(28)	(29)	(30)	(31)	(32)
Transport				Dependents				Personal					Giving					
Tickets & Passes	Vehicle tax & maintenance	Fuel	Vehicle Insurance	Care Fees	Day-to-Day Needs	Allowance	Activities	Technology	Clothing	Pastimes	Toiletries & Bodycare	Leisure	Gifts	Charity				

MONTH	YEAR

○ ....
○ ....
○ ....
○ ....
○ ....
○ ....

INCOME		OUTGOINGS	
Balance brought forward (From front page)		Expenditure (From Box A below)	
Pay 1		Mortgage or Rent	
Pay 2		Loan / Credit Card Payments	
Interest from Investments/Savings		Other	
Others		Subtotal	Box C
		To Savings 1	
		To Savings 2	
Total	Box B	Total	Box D

EXPENDITURE

Budgets →

Totals | Box A

Item	Date	Receipt?	Cleared	Household								Health				
				(1) Insurance	(2) Maintenance	(3) Utilities	(4) Cable/TV Internet/Phone	(5) Furnishings	(6) Property Tax	(7) Groceries	(8) Laundry & Cleaning	(9) Life & Health Insurance	(10) Medical, Dental & Eye Care	(11) Exercise	(12) Medicines	(13) Vacations

CALENDAR

MON	TUE	WED	THU	FRI	SAT	SUN

Transport				Dependents				Personal					Giving					
(14)	(15)	(16)	(17)	(18)	(19)	(20)	(21)	(22)	(23)	(24)	(25)	(26)	(27)	(28)	(29)	(30)	(31)	(32)
Tickets & Passes	Vehicle tax & maintenance	Fuel	Vehicle Insurance	Care Fees	Day-to-Day Needs	Allowance	Activities	Technology	Clothing	Pastimes	Toiletries & Bodycare	Leisure	Gifts	Charity				

EXPENDITURE

Item	Date	Receipt?	Cleared	Household								Health				
				(1) Insurance	(2) Maintenance	(3) Utilities	(4) Cable/TV Internet/Phone	(5) Furnishings	(6) Property Tax	(7) Groceries	(8) Laundry & Cleaning	(9) Life & Health Insurance	(10) Medical, Dental & Eye Care	(11) Exercise	(12) Medicines	(13) Vacations

(14)	(15)	(16)	(17)	(18)	(19)	(20)	(21)	(22)	(23)	(24)	(25)	(26)	(27)	(28)	(29)	(30)	(31)	(32)
Transport				Dependents				Personal					Giving					
Tickets & Passes	Vehicle tax & maintenance	Fuel	Vehicle Insurance	Care Fees	Day-to-Day Needs	Allowance	Activities	Technology	Clothing	Pastimes	Toiletries & Bodycare	Leisure	Gifts	Charity				
(14)	(15)	(16)	(17)	(18)	(19)	(20)	(21)	(22)	(23)	(24)	(25)	(26)	(27)	(28)	(29)	(30)	(31)	(32)

MONTH	YEAR

○ ....

○ ....

○ ....

○ ....

○ ....

○ ....

INCOME

Balance brought forward (From front page)	
Pay 1	
Pay 2	
Interest from Investments/Savings	
Others	
Total	Box B

OUTGOINGS

Expenditure (From Box A below)	
Mortgage or Rent	
Loan / Credit Card Payments	
Other	
Subtotal	Box C
To Savings 1	
To Savings 2	
Total	Box D

EXPENDITURE

Budgets →

Totals | Box A

			Household								Health				
Item	Date	Receipt?	Cleared	(1) Insurance	(2) Maintenance	(3) Utilities	(4) Cable/TV Internet/Phone	(5) Furnishings	(6) Property Tax	(7) Groceries	(8) Laundry & Cleaning	(9) Life & Health Insurance	(10) Medical, Dental & Eye Care	(11) Exercise	(12) Medicines	(13) Vacations

CALENDAR

MON	TUE	WED	THU	FRI	SAT	SUN

Transport				Dependents				Personal					Giving					
(14)	(15)	(16)	(17)	(18)	(19)	(20)	(21)	(22)	(23)	(24)	(25)	(26)	(27)	(28)	(29)	(30)	(31)	(32)
Tickets & Passes	Vehicle tax & maintenance	Fuel	Vehicle Insurance	Care Fees	Day-to-Day Needs	Allowance	Activities	Technology	Clothing	Pastimes	Toiletries & Bodycare	Leisure	Gifts	Charity				

EXPENDITURE

Item	Date	Receipt?	Cleared	Household								Health				
				(1) Insurance	(2) Maintenance	(3) Utilities	(4) Cable/TV Internet/Phone	(5) Furnishings	(6) Property Tax	(7) Groceries	(8) Laundry & Cleaning	(9) Life & Health Insurance	(10) Medical, Dental & Eye Care	(11) Exercise	(12) Medicines	(13) Vacations

Transport				Dependents				Personal					Giving					
(14)	(15)	(16)	(17)	(18)	(19)	(20)	(21)	(22)	(23)	(24)	(25)	(26)	(27)	(28)	(29)	(30)	(31)	(32)
Tickets & Passes	Vehicle tax & maintenance	Fuel	Vehicle Insurance	Care Fees	Day-to-Day Needs	Allowance	Activities	Technology	Clothing	Pastimes	Toiletries & Bodycare	Leisure	Gifts	Charity				

MONTH	YEAR

- ○ ....
- ○ ....
- ○ ....
- ○ ....
- ○ ....
- ○ ....

INCOME

Balance brought forward (From front page)	
Pay 1	
Pay 2	
Interest from Investments/Savings	
Others	
Total	Box B

OUTGOINGS

Expenditure (From Box A below)	
Mortgage or Rent	
Loan / Credit Card Payments	
Other	
Subtotal	Box C
To Savings 1	
To Savings 2	
Total	Box D

EXPENDITURE

Budgets →

Totals | Box A

Item	Date	Receipt?	Cleared	Household								Health				
				(1) Insurance	(2) Maintenance	(3) Utilities	(4) Cable/TV Internet/Phone	(5) Furnishings	(6) Property Tax	(7) Groceries	(8) Laundry & Cleaning	(9) Life & Health Insurance	(10) Medical, Dental & Eye Care	(11) Exercise	(12) Medicines	(13) Vacations

CALENDAR

MON	TUE	WED	THU	FRI	SAT	SUN

Transport				Dependents				Personal					Giving					
(14)	(15)	(16)	(17)	(18)	(19)	(20)	(21)	(22)	(23)	(24)	(25)	(26)	(27)	(28)	(29)	(30)	(31)	(32)
Tickets & Passes	Vehicle tax & maintenance	Fuel	Vehicle Insurance	Care Fees	Day-to-Day Needs	Allowance	Activities	Technology	Clothing	Pastimes	Toiletries & Bodycare	Leisure	Gifts	Charity				

EXPENDITURE				Household								Health				
				(1)	(2)	(3)	(4)	(5)	(6)	(7)	(8)	(9)	(10)	(11)	(12)	(13)
Item	Date	Receipt?	Cleared	Insurance	Maintenance	Utilities	Cable/TV Internet/Phone	Furnishings	Property Tax	Groceries	Laundry & Cleaning	Life & Health Insurance	Medical, Dental & Eye Care	Exercise	Medicines	Vacations

Transport				Dependents				Personal					Giving					
(14)	(15)	(16)	(17)	(18)	(19)	(20)	(21)	(22)	(23)	(24)	(25)	(26)	(27)	(28)	(29)	(30)	(31)	(32)
Tickets & Passes	Vehicle tax & maintenance	Fuel	Vehicle Insurance	Care Fees	Day-to-Day Needs	Allowance	Activities	Technology	Clothing	Pastimes	Toiletries & Bodycare	Leisure	Gifts	Charity				

MONTH	YEAR

INCOME		OUTGOINGS	
Balance brought forward (From front page)		Expenditure (From Box A below)	
Pay 1		Mortgage or Rent	
Pay 2		Loan / Credit Card Payments	
Interest from Investments/Savings		Other	
Others		Subtotal	Box C
		To Savings 1	
		To Savings 2	
Total	Box B	Total	Box D

EXPENDITURE

Budgets →

Totals | Box A

Item	Date	Receipt?	Cleared	Household								Health				
				(1)	(2)	(3)	(4)	(5)	(6)	(7)	(8)	(9)	(10)	(11)	(12)	(13)
				Insurance	Maintenance	Utilities	Cable/TV Internet/Phone	Furnishings	Property Tax	Groceries	Laundry & Cleaning	Life & Health Insurance	Medical, Dental & Eye Care	Exercise	Medicines	Vacations

CALENDAR

MON	TUE	WED	THU	FRI	SAT	SUN

Transport				Dependents				Personal					Giving					
(14)	(15)	(16)	(17)	(18)	(19)	(20)	(21)	(22)	(23)	(24)	(25)	(26)	(27)	(28)	(29)	(30)	(31)	(32)
Tickets & Passes	Vehicle tax & maintenance	Fuel	Vehicle Insurance	Care Fees	Day-to-Day Needs	Allowance	Activities	Technology	Clothing	Pastimes	Toiletries & Bodycare	Leisure	Gifts	Charity				

EXPENDITURE				Household								Health				
Item	Date	Receipt?	Cleared	(1) Insurance	(2) Maintenance	(3) Utilities	(4) Cable/TV Internet/Phone	(5) Furnishings	(6) Property Tax	(7) Groceries	(8) Laundry & Cleaning	(9) Life & Health Insurance	(10) Medical, Dental & Eye Care	(11) Exercise	(12) Medicines	(13) Vacations

	Transport			Dependents				Personal					Giving					
(14)	(15)	(16)	(17)	(18)	(19)	(20)	(21)	(22)	(23)	(24)	(25)	(26)	(27)	(28)	(29)	(30)	(31)	(32)
Tickets & Passes	Vehicle tax & maintenance	Fuel	Vehicle Insurance	Care Fees	Day-to-Day Needs	Allowance	Activities	Technology	Clothing	Pastimes	Toiletries & Bodycare	Leisure	Gifts	Charity				

MONTH	YEAR

INCOME

Balance brought forward (From front page)	
Pay 1	
Pay 2	
Interest from Investments/Savings	
Others	
Total	Box B

OUTGOINGS

Expenditure (From Box A below)	
Mortgage or Rent	
Loan / Credit Card Payments	
Other	
Subtotal	Box C
To Savings 1	
To Savings 2	
Total	Box D

EXPENDITURE

Budgets →

Totals | Box A

Item	Date	Receipt?	Cleared	(1) Insurance	(2) Maintenance	(3) Utilities	(4) Cable/TV Internet/Phone	(5) Furnishings	(6) Property Tax	(7) Groceries	(8) Laundry & Cleaning	(9) Life & Health Insurance	(10) Medical, Dental & Eye Care	(11) Exercise	(12) Medicines	(13) Vacations

Household | Health

CALENDAR

MON	TUE	WED	THU	FRI	SAT	SUN

Transport				Dependents				Personal					Giving					
(14)	(15)	(16)	(17)	(18)	(19)	(20)	(21)	(22)	(23)	(24)	(25)	(26)	(27)	(28)	(29)	(30)	(31)	(32)
Tickets & Passes	Vehicle tax & maintenance	Fuel	Vehicle Insurance	Care Fees	Day-to-Day Needs	Allowance	Activities	Technology	Clothing	Pastimes	Toiletries & Bodycare	Leisure	Gifts	Charity				

| EXPENDITURE | | | | Household | | | | | | | | Health | | | | |
Item	Date	Receipt?	Cleared	(1) Insurance	(2) Maintenance	(3) Utilities	(4) Cable/TV Internet/Phone	(5) Furnishings	(6) Property Tax	(7) Groceries	(8) Laundry & Cleaning	(9) Life & Health Insurance	(10) Medical, Dental & Eye Care	(11) Exercise	(12) Medicines	(13) Vacations

Transport				Dependents				Personal					Giving					
(14)	(15)	(16)	(17)	(18)	(19)	(20)	(21)	(22)	(23)	(24)	(25)	(26)	(27)	(28)	(29)	(30)	(31)	(32)
Tickets & Passes	Vehicle tax & maintenance	Fuel	Vehicle Insurance	Care Fees	Day-to-Day Needs	Allowance	Activities	Technology	Clothing	Pastimes	Toiletries & Bodycare	Leisure	Gifts	Charity				

MONTH	YEAR	INCOME		OUTGOINGS	
		Balance brought forward (From front page)		Expenditure (From Box A below)	
		Pay 1		Mortgage or Rent	
		Pay 2		Loan / Credit Card Payments	
		Interest from Investments/Savings		Other	
		Others		Subtotal	Box C
				To Savings 1	
				To Savings 2	
		Total	Box B	Total	Box D

EXPENDITURE

Budgets →

Totals | Box A

Item	Date	Receipt?	Cleared	Household								Health				
				(1) Insurance	(2) Maintenance	(3) Utilities	(4) Cable/TV Internet/Phone	(5) Furnishings	(6) Property Tax	(7) Groceries	(8) Laundry & Cleaning	(9) Life & Health Insurance	(10) Medical, Dental & Eye Care	(11) Exercise	(12) Medicines	(13) Vacations

CALENDAR

MON	TUE	WED	THU	FRI	SAT	SUN

Transport				Dependents				Personal					Giving					
(14)	(15)	(16)	(17)	(18)	(19)	(20)	(21)	(22)	(23)	(24)	(25)	(26)	(27)	(28)	(29)	(30)	(31)	(32)
Tickets & Passes	Vehicle tax & maintenance	Fuel	Vehicle Insurance	Care Fees	Day-to-Day Needs	Allowance	Activities	Technology	Clothing	Pastimes	Toiletries & Bodycare	Leisure	Gifts	Charity				

EXPENDITURE

Item	Date	Receipt?	Cleared	Household								Health				
				(1) Insurance	(2) Maintenance	(3) Utilities	(4) Cable/TV Internet/Phone	(5) Furnishings	(6) Property Tax	(7) Groceries	(8) Laundry & Cleaning	(9) Life & Health Insurance	(10) Medical, Dental & Eye Care	(11) Exercise	(12) Medicines	(13) Vacations

(14)	(15)	(16)	(17)	(18)	(19)	(20)	(21)	(22)	(23)	(24)	(25)	(26)	(27)	(28)	(29)	(30)	(31)	(32)
Transport				Dependents				Personal					Giving					
Tickets & Passes	Vehicle tax & maintenance	Fuel	Vehicle Insurance	Care Fees	Day-to-Day Needs	Allowance	Activities	Technology	Clothing	Pastimes	Toiletries & Bodycare	Leisure	Gifts	Charity				

MONTH	YEAR

INCOME		OUTGOINGS	
Balance brought forward (From front page)		Expenditure (From Box A below)	
Pay 1		Mortgage or Rent	
Pay 2		Loan / Credit Card Payments	
Interest from Investments/Savings		Other	
Others		Subtotal	Box C
		To Savings 1	
		To Savings 2	
	Total	Box B	Total	Box D

○ _____
○ _____
○ _____
○ _____
○ _____
○ _____

EXPENDITURE

Budgets →

Totals | Box A |

Item	Date	Receipt?	Cleared	Household								Health				
				(1)	(2)	(3)	(4)	(5)	(6)	(7)	(8)	(9)	(10)	(11)	(12)	(13)
				Insurance	Maintenance	Utilities	Cable/TV Internet/Phone	Furnishings	Property Tax	Groceries	Laundry & Cleaning	Life & Health Insurance	Medical, Dental & Eye Care	Exercise	Medicines	Vacations

CALENDAR

MON	TUE	WED	THU	FRI	SAT	SUN

Transport				Dependents				Personal					Giving					
(14)	(15)	(16)	(17)	(18)	(19)	(20)	(21)	(22)	(23)	(24)	(25)	(26)	(27)	(28)	(29)	(30)	(31)	(32)
Tickets & Passes	Vehicle tax & maintenance	Fuel	Vehicle Insurance	Care Fees	Day-to-Day Needs	Allowance	Activities	Technology	Clothing	Pastimes	Toiletries & Bodycare	Leisure	Gifts	Charity				

EXPENDITURE

Item	Date	Receipt?	Cleared	Household								Health				
				(1) Insurance	(2) Maintenance	(3) Utilities	(4) Cable/TV Internet/Phone	(5) Furnishings	(6) Property Tax	(7) Groceries	(8) Laundry & Cleaning	(9) Life & Health Insurance	(10) Medical, Dental & Eye Care	(11) Exercise	(12) Medicines	(13) Vacations

Transport				Dependents				Personal					Giving					
(14)	(15)	(16)	(17)	(18)	(19)	(20)	(21)	(22)	(23)	(24)	(25)	(26)	(27)	(28)	(29)	(30)	(31)	(32)
Tickets & Passes	Vehicle tax & maintenance	Fuel	Vehicle Insurance	Care Fees	Day-to-Day Needs	Allowance	Activities	Technology	Clothing	Pastimes	Toiletries & Bodycare	Leisure	Gifts	Charity				

MONTH	YEAR

INCOME		OUTGOINGS	
Balance brought forward (From front page)		Expenditure (From Box A below)	
Pay 1		Mortgage or Rent	
Pay 2		Loan / Credit Card Payments	
Interest from Investments/Savings		Other	
Others		Subtotal	Box C
		To Savings 1	
		To Savings 2	
Total	Box B	Total	Box D

EXPENDITURE

Budgets →

Totals | Box A

Item	Date	Receipt?	Cleared	Household								Health				
				(1)	(2)	(3)	(4)	(5)	(6)	(7)	(8)	(9)	(10)	(11)	(12)	(13)
				Insurance	Maintenance	Utilities	Cable/TV Internet/Phone	Furnishings	Property Tax	Groceries	Laundry & Cleaning	Life & Health Insurance	Medical, Dental & Eye Care	Exercise	Medicines	Vacations

CALENDAR

MON	TUE	WED	THU	FRI	SAT	SUN

Transport				Dependents				Personal					Giving					
(14)	(15)	(16)	(17)	(18)	(19)	(20)	(21)	(22)	(23)	(24)	(25)	(26)	(27)	(28)	(29)	(30)	(31)	(32)
Tickets & Passes	Vehicle tax & maintenance	Fuel	Vehicle Insurance	Care Fees	Day-to-Day Needs	Allowance	Activities	Technology	Clothing	Pastimes	Toiletries & Bodycare	Leisure	Gifts	Charity				

EXPENDITURE

Item	Date	Receipt?	Cleared	Household								Health				
				(1) Insurance	(2) Maintenance	(3) Utilities	(4) Cable/TV Internet/Phone	(5) Furnishings	(6) Property Tax	(7) Groceries	(8) Laundry & Cleaning	(9) Life & Health Insurance	(10) Medical, Dental & Eye Care	(11) Exercise	(12) Medicines	(13) Vacations

(14)	(15)	(16)	(17)	(18)	(19)	(20)	(21)	(22)	(23)	(24)	(25)	(26)	(27)	(28)	(29)	(30)	(31)	(32)
Transport				Dependents				Personal					Giving					
Tickets & Passes	Vehicle tax & maintenance	Fuel	Vehicle Insurance	Care Fees	Day-to-Day Needs	Allowance	Activities	Technology	Clothing	Pastimes	Toiletries & Bodycare	Leisure	Gifts	Charity				
(14)	(15)	(16)	(17)	(18)	(19)	(20)	(21)	(22)	(23)	(24)	(25)	(26)	(27)	(28)	(29)	(30)	(31)	(32)

MONTH	YEAR

○	
○	
○	
○	
○	
○	

INCOME

Balance brought forward (From front page)	
Pay 1	
Pay 2	
Interest from Investments/Savings	
Others	
Total	Box B

OUTGOINGS

Expenditure (From Box A below)	
Mortgage or Rent	
Loan / Credit Card Payments	
Other	
Subtotal	Box C
To Savings 1	
To Savings 2	
Total	Box D

EXPENDITURE

Budgets →

Totals | Box A

	Household								Health				
	(1)	(2)	(3)	(4)	(5)	(6)	(7)	(8)	(9)	(10)	(11)	(12)	(13)
Item / Date / Receipt? / Cleared	Insurance	Maintenance	Utilities	Cable/TV Internet/Phone	Furnishings	Property Tax	Groceries	Laundry & Cleaning	Life & Health Insurance	Medical, Dental & Eye Care	Exercise	Medicines	Vacations

CALENDAR

MON	TUE	WED	THU	FRI	SAT	SUN

Transport				Dependents				Personal					Giving					
(14)	(15)	(16)	(17)	(18)	(19)	(20)	(21)	(22)	(23)	(24)	(25)	(26)	(27)	(28)	(29)	(30)	(31)	(32)
Tickets & Passes	Vehicle tax & maintenance	Fuel	Vehicle Insurance	Care Fees	Day-to-Day Needs	Allowance	Activities	Technology	Clothing	Pastimes	Toiletries & Bodycare	Leisure	Gifts	Charity				

EXPENDITURE				Household								Health				
Item	Date	Receipt?	Cleared	(1) Insurance	(2) Maintenance	(3) Utilities	(4) Cable/TV Internet/Phone	(5) Furnishings	(6) Property Tax	(7) Groceries	(8) Laundry & Cleaning	(9) Life & Health Insurance	(10) Medical, Dental & Eye Care	(11) Exercise	(12) Medicines	(13) Vacations

Transport				Dependents				Personal					Giving				
(14)	(15)	(16)	(17)	(18)	(19)	(20)	(21)	(22)	(23)	(24)	(25)	(26)	(27)	(28)	(29)	(30)	(31)	(32)
Tickets & Passes	Vehicle tax & maintenance	Fuel	Vehicle Insurance	Care Fees	Day-to-Day Needs	Allowance	Activities	Technology	Clothing	Pastimes	Toiletries & Bodycare	Leisure	Gifts	Charity				

MONTH	YEAR

- _____
- _____
- _____
- _____
- _____
- _____

INCOME

Balance brought forward (From front page)	
Pay 1	
Pay 2	
Interest from Investments/Savings	
Others	
Total	Box B

OUTGOINGS

Expenditure (From Box A below)	
Mortgage or Rent	
Loan / Credit Card Payments	
Other	
Subtotal	Box C
To Savings 1	
To Savings 2	
Total	Box D

EXPENDITURE

Budgets →

Totals | Box A

Item	Date	Receipt?	Cleared	(1) Insurance	(2) Maintenance	(3) Utilities	(4) Cable/TV Internet/Phone	(5) Furnishings	(6) Property Tax	(7) Groceries	(8) Laundry & Cleaning	(9) Life & Health Insurance	(10) Medical, Dental & Eye Care	(11) Exercise	(12) Medicines	(13) Vacations

Household — columns (1)–(8)

Health — columns (9)–(13)

CALENDAR

MON	TUE	WED	THU	FRI	SAT	SUN

Transport				Dependents				Personal					Giving					
(14)	(15)	(16)	(17)	(18)	(19)	(20)	(21)	(22)	(23)	(24)	(25)	(26)	(27)	(28)	(29)	(30)	(31)	(32)
Tickets & Passes	Vehicle tax & maintenance	Fuel	Vehicle Insurance	Care Fees	Day-to-Day Needs	Allowance	Activities	Technology	Clothing	Pastimes	Toiletries & Bodycare	Leisure	Gifts	Charity				

Item	Date	Receipt?	Cleared	Household								Health				
				(1) Insurance	(2) Maintenance	(3) Utilities	(4) Cable/TV Internet/Phone	(5) Furnishings	(6) Property Tax	(7) Groceries	(8) Laundry & Cleaning	(9) Life & Health Insurance	(10) Medical, Dental & Eye Care	(11) Exercise	(12) Medicines	(13) Vacations

(14)	(15)	(16)	(17)	(18)	(19)	(20)	(21)	(22)	(23)	(24)	(25)	(26)	(27)	(28)	(29)	(30)	(31)	(32)
Transport				Dependents				Personal					Giving					
Tickets & Passes	Vehicle tax & maintenance	Fuel	Vehicle Insurance	Care Fees	Day-to-Day Needs	Allowance	Activities	Technology	Clothing	Pastimes	Toiletries & Bodycare	Leisure	Gifts	Charity				
Transport				Dependents				Personal					Giving					

MONTH	YEAR

INCOME		OUTGOINGS	
Balance brought forward (From front page)		Expenditure (From Box A below)	
Pay 1		Mortgage or Rent	
Pay 2		Loan / Credit Card Payments	
Interest from Investments/Savings		Other	
Others		Subtotal	Box C
		To Savings 1	
		To Savings 2	
Total	Box B	Total	Box D

EXPENDITURE

Budgets →

Totals | Box A

Item	Date	Receipt?	Cleared	Household								Health				
				(1) Insurance	(2) Maintenance	(3) Utilities	(4) Cable/TV Internet/Phone	(5) Furnishings	(6) Property Tax	(7) Groceries	(8) Laundry & Cleaning	(9) Life & Health Insurance	(10) Medical, Dental & Eye Care	(11) Exercise	(12) Medicines	(13) Vacations

CALENDAR

MON	TUE	WED	THU	FRI	SAT	SUN

Transport				Dependents				Personal					Giving					
(14)	(15)	(16)	(17)	(18)	(19)	(20)	(21)	(22)	(23)	(24)	(25)	(26)	(27)	(28)	(29)	(30)	(31)	(32)
Tickets & Passes	Vehicle tax & maintenance	Fuel	Vehicle Insurance	Care Fees	Day-to-Day Needs	Allowance	Activities	Technology	Clothing	Pastimes	Toiletries & Bodycare	Leisure	Gifts	Charity				

EXPENDITURE				Household								Health				
Item	Date	Receipt?	Cleared	(1) Insurance	(2) Maintenance	(3) Utilities	(4) Cable/TV Internet/Phone	(5) Furnishings	(6) Property Tax	(7) Groceries	(8) Laundry & Cleaning	(9) Life & Health Insurance	(10) Medical, Dental & Eye Care	(11) Exercise	(12) Medicines	(13) Vacations

	Transport			Dependents				Personal						Giving					
(14)	(15)	(16)	(17)	(18)	(19)	(20)	(21)	(22)	(23)	(24)	(25)	(26)	(27)	(28)	(29)	(30)	(31)	(32)
Tickets & Passes	Vehicle tax & maintenance	Fuel	Vehicle Insurance	Care Fees	Day-to-Day Needs	Allowance	Activities	Technology	Clothing	Pastimes	Toiletries & Bodycare	Leisure	Gifts	Charity				

MONTH	YEAR

- ○ ....
- ○ ....
- ○ ....
- ○ ....
- ○ ....
- ○ ....

INCOME

Balance brought forward (From front page)	
Pay 1	
Pay 2	
Interest from Investments/Savings	
Others	
Total	Box B

OUTGOINGS

Expenditure (From Box A below)	
Mortgage or Rent	
Loan / Credit Card Payments	
Other	
Subtotal	Box C
To Savings 1	
To Savings 2	
Total	Box D

EXPENDITURE

Budgets →

Totals | Box A

Item	Date	Receipt?	Cleared	Household								Health				
				(1) Insurance	(2) Maintenance	(3) Utilities	(4) Cable/TV Internet/Phone	(5) Furnishings	(6) Property Tax	(7) Groceries	(8) Laundry & Cleaning	(9) Life & Health Insurance	(10) Medical, Dental & Eye Care	(11) Exercise	(12) Medicines	(13) Vacations

CALENDAR

MON	TUE	WED	THU	FRI	SAT	SUN

Transport				Dependents				Personal					Giving					
(14)	(15)	(16)	(17)	(18)	(19)	(20)	(21)	(22)	(23)	(24)	(25)	(26)	(27)	(28)	(29)	(30)	(31)	(32)
Tickets & Passes	Vehicle tax & maintenance	Fuel	Vehicle Insurance	Care Fees	Day-to-Day Needs	Allowance	Activities	Technology	Clothing	Pastimes	Toiletries & Bodycare	Leisure	Gifts	Charity				

EXPENDITURE

Item	Date	Receipt?	Cleared	Household								Health				
				(1) Insurance	(2) Maintenance	(3) Utilities	(4) Cable/TV Internet/Phone	(5) Furnishings	(6) Property Tax	(7) Groceries	(8) Laundry & Cleaning	(9) Life & Health Insurance	(10) Medical, Dental & Eye Care	(11) Exercise	(12) Medicines	(13) Vacations

Transport				Dependents				Personal					Giving					
(14)	(15)	(16)	(17)	(18)	(19)	(20)	(21)	(22)	(23)	(24)	(25)	(26)	(27)	(28)	(29)	(30)	(31)	(32)
Tickets & Passes	Vehicle tax & maintenance	Fuel	Vehicle Insurance	Care Fees	Day-to-Day Needs	Allowance	Activities	Technology	Clothing	Pastimes	Toiletries & Bodycare	Leisure	Gifts	Charity				
(14)	(15)	(16)	(17)	(18)	(19)	(20)	(21)	(22)	(23)	(24)	(25)	(26)	(27)	(28)	(29)	(30)	(31)	(32)

MONTH	YEAR

INCOME		OUTGOINGS	
Balance brought forward (From front page)		Expenditure (From Box A below)	
Pay 1		Mortgage or Rent	
Pay 2		Loan / Credit Card Payments	
Interest from Investments/Savings		Other	
Others		Subtotal	Box C
		To Savings 1	
		To Savings 2	
Total	Box B	Total	Box D

○ _____
○ _____
○ _____
○ _____
○ _____
○ _____

EXPENDITURE

Budgets →

Totals | Box A

Item	Date	Receipt?	Cleared	Household								Health				
				(1) Insurance	(2) Maintenance	(3) Utilities	(4) Cable/TV Internet/Phone	(5) Furnishings	(6) Property Tax	(7) Groceries	(8) Laundry & Cleaning	(9) Life & Health Insurance	(10) Medical, Dental & Eye Care	(11) Exercise	(12) Medicines	(13) Vacations

CALENDAR

MON	TUE	WED	THU	FRI	SAT	SUN

Transport				Dependents				Personal					Giving					
(14)	(15)	(16)	(17)	(18)	(19)	(20)	(21)	(22)	(23)	(24)	(25)	(26)	(27)	(28)	(29)	(30)	(31)	(32)
Tickets & Passes	Vehicle tax & maintenance	Fuel	Vehicle Insurance	Care Fees	Day-to-Day Needs	Allowance	Activities	Technology	Clothing	Pastimes	Toiletries & Bodycare	Leisure	Gifts	Charity				

| EXPENDITURE | | | | Household | | | | | | | | Health | | | | |
Item	Date	Receipt?	Cleared	Insurance (1)	Maintenance (2)	Utilities (3)	Cable/TV Internet/Phone (4)	Furnishings (5)	Property Tax (6)	Groceries (7)	Laundry & Cleaning (8)	Life & Health Insurance (9)	Medical, Dental & Eye Care (10)	Exercise (11)	Medicines (12)	Vacations (13)

(14)	(15)	(16)	(17)	(18)	(19)	(20)	(21)	(22)	(23)	(24)	(25)	(26)	(27)	(28)	(29)	(30)	(31)	(32)
Transport				Dependents				Personal					Giving					
Tickets & Passes	Vehicle tax & maintenance	Fuel	Vehicle Insurance	Care Fees	Day-to-Day Needs	Allowance	Activities	Technology	Clothing	Pastimes	Toiletries & Bodycare	Leisure	Gifts	Charity				

MONTH	YEAR

INCOME		OUTGOINGS	
Balance brought forward (From front page)		Expenditure (From Box A below)	
Pay 1		Mortgage or Rent	
Pay 2		Loan / Credit Card Payments	
Interest from Investments/Savings		Other	
Others		Subtotal	Box C
		To Savings 1	
		To Savings 2	
Total	Box B	Total	Box D

EXPENDITURE

Budgets →

Totals | Box A

Item	Date	Receipt?	Cleared	Household								Health				
				(1) Insurance	(2) Maintenance	(3) Utilities	(4) Cable/TV Internet/Phone	(5) Furnishings	(6) Property Tax	(7) Groceries	(8) Laundry & Cleaning	(9) Life & Health Insurance	(10) Medical, Dental & Eye Care	(11) Exercise	(12) Medicines	(13) Vacations

CALENDAR

MON	TUE	WED	THU	FRI	SAT	SUN

Transport				Dependents				Personal					Giving					
(14)	(15)	(16)	(17)	(18)	(19)	(20)	(21)	(22)	(23)	(24)	(25)	(26)	(27)	(28)	(29)	(30)	(31)	(32)
Tickets & Passes	Vehicle tax & maintenance	Fuel	Vehicle Insurance	Care Fees	Day-to-Day Needs	Allowance	Activities	Technology	Clothing	Pastimes	Toiletries & Bodycare	Leisure	Gifts	Charity				

EXPENDITURE				Household								Health				
Item	Date	Receipt?	Cleared	(1) Insurance	(2) Maintenance	(3) Utilities	(4) Cable/TV Internet/Phone	(5) Furnishings	(6) Property Tax	(7) Groceries	(8) Laundry & Cleaning	(9) Life & Health Insurance	(10) Medical, Dental & Eye Care	(11) Exercise	(12) Medicines	(13) Vacations

Transport				Dependents				Personal					Giving					
(14)	(15)	(16)	(17)	(18)	(19)	(20)	(21)	(22)	(23)	(24)	(25)	(26)	(27)	(28)	(29)	(30)	(31)	(32)
Tickets & Passes	Vehicle tax & maintenance	Fuel	Vehicle Insurance	Care Fees	Day-to-Day Needs	Allowance	Activities	Technology	Clothing	Pastimes	Toiletries & Bodycare	Leisure	Gifts	Charity				

MONTH	YEAR

INCOME		OUTGOINGS	
Balance brought forward (From front page)		Expenditure (From Box A below)	
Pay 1		Mortgage or Rent	
Pay 2		Loan / Credit Card Payments	
Interest from Investments/Savings		Other	
Others		Subtotal	Box C
		To Savings 1	
		To Savings 2	
Total	Box B	Total	Box D

EXPENDITURE

Budgets →

Totals | Box A

Item	Date	Receipt?	Cleared	Household								Health				
				(1) Insurance	(2) Maintenance	(3) Utilities	(4) Cable/TV Internet/Phone	(5) Furnishings	(6) Property Tax	(7) Groceries	(8) Laundry & Cleaning	(9) Life & Health Insurance	(10) Medical, Dental & Eye Care	(11) Exercise	(12) Medicines	(13) Vacations

CALENDAR

MON	TUE	WED	THU	FRI	SAT	SUN

Transport				Dependents				Personal					Giving					
(14)	(15)	(16)	(17)	(18)	(19)	(20)	(21)	(22)	(23)	(24)	(25)	(26)	(27)	(28)	(29)	(30)	(31)	(32)
Tickets & Passes	Vehicle tax & maintenance	Fuel	Vehicle Insurance	Care Fees	Day-to-Day Needs	Allowance	Activities	Technology	Clothing	Pastimes	Toiletries & Bodycare	Leisure	Gifts	Charity				

EXPENDITURE				Household								Health				
				(1)	(2)	(3)	(4)	(5)	(6)	(7)	(8)	(9)	(10)	(11)	(12)	(13)
Item	Date	Receipt?	Cleared	Insurance	Maintenance	Utilities	Cable/TV Internet/Phone	Furnishings	Property Tax	Groceries	Laundry & Cleaning	Life & Health Insurance	Medical, Dental & Eye Care	Exercise	Medicines	Vacations

Transport				Dependents				Personal					Giving					
(14)	(15)	(16)	(17)	(18)	(19)	(20)	(21)	(22)	(23)	(24)	(25)	(26)	(27)	(28)	(29)	(30)	(31)	(32)
Tickets & Passes	Vehicle tax & maintenance	Fuel	Vehicle Insurance	Care Fees	Day-to-Day Needs	Allowance	Activities	Technology	Clothing	Pastimes	Toiletries & Bodycare	Leisure	Gifts	Charity				

MONTH	YEAR

- ○ _____
- ○ _____
- ○ _____
- ○ _____
- ○ _____
- ○ _____

INCOME

Balance brought forward (From front page)	
Pay 1	
Pay 2	
Interest from Investments/Savings	
Others	
Total	Box B

OUTGOINGS

Expenditure (From Box A below)	
Mortgage or Rent	
Loan / Credit Card Payments	
Other	
Subtotal	Box C
To Savings 1	
To Savings 2	
Total	Box D

EXPENDITURE

Budgets →

Totals | Box A

Item	Date	Receipt?	Cleared	(1) Insurance	(2) Maintenance	(3) Utilities	(4) Cable/TV Internet/Phone	(5) Furnishings	(6) Property Tax	(7) Groceries	(8) Laundry & Cleaning	(9) Life & Health Insurance	(10) Medical, Dental & Eye Care	(11) Exercise	(12) Medicines	(13) Vacations

Household | Health

CALENDAR

MON	TUE	WED	THU	FRI	SAT	SUN

Transport				Dependents				Personal					Giving					
(14)	(15)	(16)	(17)	(18)	(19)	(20)	(21)	(22)	(23)	(24)	(25)	(26)	(27)	(28)	(29)	(30)	(31)	(32)
Tickets & Passes	Vehicle tax & maintenance	Fuel	Vehicle Insurance	Care Fees	Day-to-Day Needs	Allowance	Activities	Technology	Clothing	Pastimes	Toiletries & Bodycare	Leisure	Gifts	Charity				

EXPENDITURE				Household								Health				
Item	Date	Receipt?	Cleared	(1) Insurance	(2) Maintenance	(3) Utilities	(4) Cable/TV Internet/Phone	(5) Furnishings	(6) Property Tax	(7) Groceries	(8) Laundry & Cleaning	(9) Life & Health Insurance	(10) Medical, Dental & Eye Care	(11) Exercise	(12) Medicines	(13) Vacations

(14)	(15)	(16)	(17)	(18)	(19)	(20)	(21)	(22)	(23)	(24)	(25)	(26)	(27)	(28)	(29)	(30)	(31)	(32)
Transport				Dependents				Personal					Giving					
Tickets & Passes	Vehicle tax & maintenance	Fuel	Vehicle Insurance	Care Fees	Day-to-Day Needs	Allowance	Activities	Technology	Clothing	Pastimes	Toiletries & Bodycare	Leisure	Gifts	Charity				

MONTH	YEAR

INCOME		OUTGOINGS	
Balance brought forward (From front page)		Expenditure (From Box A below)	
Pay 1		Mortgage or Rent	
Pay 2		Loan / Credit Card Payments	
Interest from Investments/Savings		Other	
Others		Subtotal	Box C
		To Savings 1	
		To Savings 2	
	Total	Box B	Total	Box D

EXPENDITURE				Household								Health				
Budgets →																
Totals	Box A															
				(1)	(2)	(3)	(4)	(5)	(6)	(7)	(8)	(9)	(10)	(11)	(12)	(13)
Item	Date	Receipt?	Cleared	Insurance	Maintenance	Utilities	Cable/TV Internet/Phone	Furnishings	Property Tax	Groceries	Laundry & Cleaning	Life & Health Insurance	Medical, Dental & Eye Care	Exercise	Medicines	Vacations

CALENDAR

MON	TUE	WED	THU	FRI	SAT	SUN

Transport				Dependents				Personal					Giving					
(14)	(15)	(16)	(17)	(18)	(19)	(20)	(21)	(22)	(23)	(24)	(25)	(26)	(27)	(28)	(29)	(30)	(31)	(32)
Tickets & Passes	Vehicle tax & maintenance	Fuel	Vehicle Insurance	Care Fees	Day-to-Day Needs	Allowance	Activities	Technology	Clothing	Pastimes	Toiletries & Bodycare	Leisure	Gifts	Charity				

EXPENDITURE				Household								Health				
				(1)	(2)	(3)	(4)	(5)	(6)	(7)	(8)	(9)	(10)	(11)	(12)	(13)
Item	Date	Receipt?	Cleared	Insurance	Maintenance	Utilities	Cable/TV Internet/Phone	Furnishings	Property Tax	Groceries	Laundry & Cleaning	Life & Health Insurance	Medical, Dental & Eye Care	Exercise	Medicines	Vacations

(14)	(15)	(16)	(17)	(18)	(19)	(20)	(21)	(22)	(23)	(24)	(25)	(26)	(27)	(28)	(29)	(30)	(31)	(32)
Transport				Dependents				Personal					Giving					
Tickets & Passes	Vehicle tax & maintenance	Fuel	Vehicle Insurance	Care Fees	Day-to-Day Needs	Allowance	Activities	Technology	Clothing	Pastimes	Toiletries & Bodycare	Leisure	Gifts	Charity				

SAVINGS LOG 1

Saving for: _____ Target: _____

Date	Description	In	Out *	Balance

SAVINGS LOG 2

Saving for: _____ Target: _____

Date	Description	In	Out *	Balance

* When you make purchases from these Savings Logs, do not enter them in your monthly expenditure charts.

NOTES

Manufactured by Amazon.ca
Bolton, ON

31259863R00057